THE
JOKIEST
JOKING
RIDDLES BOOK
EVER WRITTEN . . . NO JOKE!

LOOKING FOR MORE JOKES TO IMPRESS YOUR FRIENDS AND
BUILD YOUR ULTIMATE JOKEMASTER COLLECTION?

YOU'LL LOVE...

**THE JOKIEST JOKING JOKE BOOK EVER WRITTEN
. . . NO JOKE!**

**THE JOKIEST JOKING KNOCK-KNOCK JOKE BOOK
EVER WRITTEN . . . NO JOKE!**

**THE JOKIEST JOKING TRIVIA BOOK EVER WRITTEN
. . . NO JOKE!**

**THE JOKIEST JOKING BATHROOM JOKE BOOK EVER WRITTEN
. . . NO JOKE!**

**THE JOKIEST JOKING PUNS BOOK EVER WRITTEN
. . . NO JOKE!**

**THE ULTIMATE JOKIEST JOKING JOKE BOOK EVER
. . . NO JOKE!**

THE
JOKIEST
JOKING
RIDDLES BOOK
EVER WRITTEN ... NO JOKE!

1,001 ALL-NEW BRAIN TEASERS THAT WILL KEEP YOU LAUGHING OUT LOUD

Jokes by Brian Boone

Illustrations by Amanda Brack

CASTLE POINT BOOKS
NEW YORK

THE JOKIEST JOKING RIDDLES BOOK EVER WRITTEN . . . NO JOKE!

Copyright © 2020 by St. Martin's Press.

All rights reserved.

Printed in the United States of America.

For information, address St. Martin's Publishing Group,

120 Broadway, New York, NY 10271

www.castlepointbooks.com

The Castle Point Books trademark is owned by Castle Point Publishing, LLC.
Castle Point books are published and distributed by St. Martin's Press.

The Library of Congress Cataloging-in-Publication Data is available upon
request.

ISBN 978-1-250-24047-7 (trade paperback)
ISBN 978-1-250-24105-4 (ebook)

Our books may be purchased in bulk for promotional, educational, or
business use. Please contact your local bookseller or the Macmillan
Corporate and Premium Sales Department at 1-800-221-7945, extension
5442, or by email at MacmillanSpecialMarkets@macmillan.com.

First Edition: March 2020

10 9 8 7 6 5 4 3 2 1

CONTENTS

When is a joke not a joke, but also a joke? Give up? When it's a riddle. See? That right there was a riddle!

A riddle is a different kind of joke. Sure, riddles are just like puns, knock-knock jokes, or a story-style joke in that they've got a thoughtful setup and then a punch line . . . which results in either a joyful, surprising outburst of laughter or a good-natured groan, if it's a really bad joke. But riddles are also nothing like those other familiar kinds of jokes because they're all about cleverness and smarts. They're jokes you can solve—or guess the punch line to beforehand—with just a little bit of thought and craftiness. They won't always make you laugh out loud, but they are always amusing and always fun.

Want to hear another riddle? Sure you do. What do you hold in your hands right now that you may not even realize? Hundreds upon hundreds of the best riddles of all time. They're right here waiting to peel the ol' brain banana, covering every page of *The Jokiest Joking Riddles Book Ever Written . . . No Joke!*

So when you read these riddles, try not to jump to the answer right away. Or, if you're telling these to other people, give them a moment to think it through. A little logic just might get you to the answer. You'll feel smart, you'll be entertained, and you'll say, "Ah, I knew it!"

Riddles are the perfect joke!

1
WILD KINGDOM

**Creature Features to Teach You,
We Beseech You!**

What fish don't swim?
Dead fish.

**I stay alive without breathing air.
I'm rarely thirsty but always have plenty
of water.
What am I?**

A fish.

**Thousands fill this house with gold,
but no man made this house.
It's guarded by its spear-wielding residents.
What is it?**

A beehive.

**I am a country, a bird, and sometimes also cold.
What am I?**

Turkey.

What goes 99 thump, 99 thump, 99 thump?

A centipede with a wooden leg.

Why does a dog wag its tail?

Nobody else will wag it for him.

What's small, fuzzy, and can't breathe?

A koala holding its breath.

What animal never gets hungry and never needs to eat?
Stuffed animals.

Jack and Jill lay dead on the floor. There's shattered glass next to them, and they died from a lack of water. What happened?
They're goldfish.

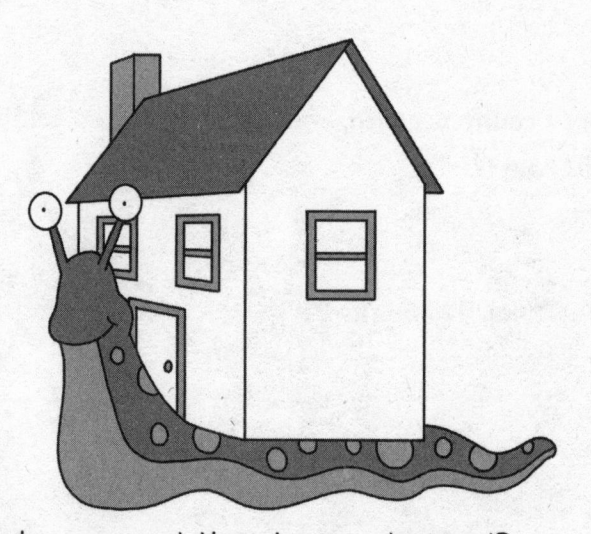

Why is a snail the strongest animal? It carries its house on its back.

A house has four walls, and they all face south. A bear sits outside. What color is the bear?

White. It's a polar bear because the house is at the North Pole.

What's key to a great Thanksgiving?

A turkey.

What kind of key can open a church?

A monkey.

What has twelve legs, six eyes, and can't see?
Three Blind Mice.

What's smarter than a talking bird?
A spelling bee.

What's worse than finding a worm in your apple?

Finding half a worm in your apple.

What's the number one use of cowhide?

Holding cows together.

Why do bears have fur coats?

Because they don't have money to buy jackets.

Why do hummingbirds hum?

Because they don't know the words.

What's out of bounds?
A tired kangaroo.

How do you make a ponytail?

Make up a story about a horse.

Why did the turkey cross the road?

It wasn't chicken!

Why do dogs run in circles?

Because they can't run around in triangles.

Why did the bird fall out of the tree?

Because it was dead.

I live with hundreds of my brothers and one lovely lady, but she's not my honey.
What am I?
A bee.

What time is it when 10 lions are chasing you?
10 after 1.

Why does a chicken coop have two doors?
Because if it had four, it would be a sedan.

How do you make a goldfish old?
Take away the "g."

What's the most musical part of a turkey?
Its drumsticks.

**I'm made of gold yet have no money
(and cost almost nothing).
What am I?**

A goldfish.

**I jump when I walk, and I sit when I stand.
What am I?**

A kangaroo.

**I always go to bed with my shoes on.
What am I?**

A horse.

I have eyes in my head, but many more on my tail.

What am I?

A peacock.

100 feet in the air, back on the ground.

What am I?

A centipede . . . lying on its back.

How do you make any dog into a Scotty dog?

Rename it Scotty.

When is fishing not relaxing?
When you're a worm!

What asks but never answers?

An owl.

What's smaller than an ant's mouth?

Whatever an ant eats.

HER: I want to buy a dog, but they're so expensive.
Do you know of any that go cheap?
HIM: No, most dogs bark.

How do you avoid diseases from biting insects?

Don't bite insects.

I'm a celebrity fish but am neither celebrity nor fish.
What am I?
A starfish.

What do zebras have that no other animals have?

Zebra babies.

Why does a giraffe have such a long neck?

Because its head is very far away from its body.

When is it truly unlucky for a black cat to cross your path?

If you're a mouse.

How is an old dog like a hill?

One is a slow pup, the other is a slope up.

Why does a flamingo stand on one leg?
If it lifted up that leg, it would fall down.

How do you spell cat backwards?

C-A-T-B-A-C-K-W-A-R-D-S

What does a dog do but a person wears?

Pants!

How do you cure a dog's fleas?

Depends on what sickness the fleas have.

Why did the deer eat raw grass?

Because it never learned how to cook it.

What bird can lift the most?
The crane.

Why do birds fly south for the winter?

Because it's easier than walking.

Where do birds go to school?

High school.

What is the best way to stop a dog from barking in, and digging up, the front yard?

Put it in the backyard.

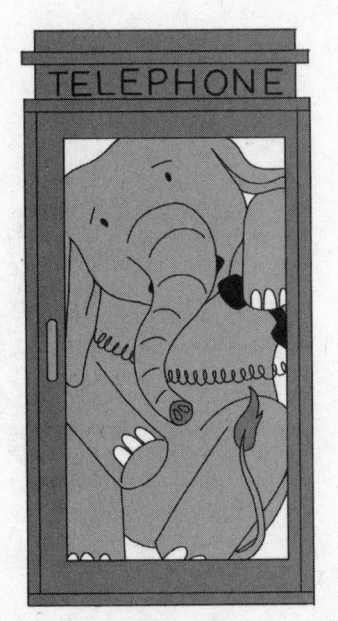

What do you call an elephant in a phone booth?
Stuck!

What would you do if a giraffe sat in front of you at a movie?

Miss most of the movie.

Why does a hippo drink more water in August than in September?

Because there are more days in August.

Why was the dog allowed at school?

Because she was the teacher's pet.

Why do gorillas have big nostrils?
Because they have big fingers.

Why are elephants so wrinkled?

Because they're really hard to iron.

**What does a baby duck become
when it goes into the water for the first time?**

Wet!

Can a dog on a 10-foot leash walk 20 feet away?

Sure, if you aren't holding the leash.

What horse has six legs?

One that's being ridden.

What kind of fish belongs in a birdcage?
Perch.

How many horses have three legs?

All of them.

How does a dead skunk smell?

Awful!

Why do white sheep eat more than black sheep?

There are more of them in the world.

What are the laziest pets you can have?

Carpets.

Where does a frog sit?
On a toadstool.

What are the most musical pets?

Trumpets.

What do cats and dogs have in common?

"S."

What grows up while growing down?

A goose.

What do you call a bird in the winter?
A brrr-d!

**I have no eyes, no legs, and no ears,
but I'm strong enough to move the earth. What am I?**

A worm.

What animal makes the most of its food?

A giraffe. It makes a little go a long way.

If all the cows talked at once, what would they say?

Nothing—cows can't talk.

Why do cows wear bells?

Because their horns don't work.

What does a very, very bad hen lay?
Deviled eggs.

What lives in pens but isn't ink?

Pigs!

What did the bee say when it returned to the hive?

"Honey. I'm home!"

What do you call a one-winged fly?

A walk.

What do you call a snail without its shell?

A slug.

Why do male deer need braces?
Because they have buck teeth!

How do pigs write?

With a pigpen.

How is a fish like a blabbermouth?

Neither can keep their mouth shut.

If there was an egg in the middle of space,
where did it come from?

A chicken.

What does a triceratops sit on?
Its tricera-bottom!

Why do dogs hate clocks?
The ticks.

What kind of gun shoots insects?
A bee-bee gun.

**Every morning a farmer ate eggs,
but he didn't have chickens on his farm.
Where did he get those eggs?**
From his ducks.

What animals walk everywhere you go?
Calves.

What has 50 legs but can't walk?
Half of a centipede.

What horses stay up late?
Nightmares.

Why does the ocean roar?
It has crabs in its bed.

What does a mixed-up hen lay?
Scrambled eggs!

What animal keeps the best time?
A watch dog.

What color socks do bears wear?

They don't wear socks—they have bear feet.

What's black and white,
black and white,
and black and white?

A panda bear rolling down a hill.

What's black and white and red all over?

A panda bear with a sunburn.

Why did the snowman call his dog "Frost"?
Because Frost bites.

How do you make a gummy bear?

Remove the bear's teeth.

Why do seagulls fly over the sea?

Because if they flew over the bay, they'd be called bagels!

What bird is with you at every meal?

A swallow.

How do you grow a bird?

With bird seed.

Two flies are on a porch.
Which one is the actor?
The one on the screen.

How do chickens bake a cake?
From scratch.

What do you call a dinosaur that never gives up?
A try-try-try-ceratops!

What do you call a sick pony?
A little hoarse.

What do you call a dinosaur that smashes everything in its path?

Tyrannosaurus wrecks!

What do you do if you find a blue parrot?

Cheer him up!

Why don't dinosaurs ever forget?

Because no one ever bothers to tell them anything.

What do you need to know to teach a dinosaur tricks?

More than the dinosaur knows.

Where was the dinosaur when the sun went down?

In the dark!

Why didn't the dinosaur cross the road?

There weren't any roads back then!

Why did dinosaurs eat raw meat?

Because they didn't know how to cook.

Why did the terrier bite the woman's ankle?

Because she couldn't reach any higher.

What's the most talkative animal?
The yak.

Why do you need a license for a dog and not for a cat?

Cats can't drive!

What do you call a stubborn dog?

It doesn't matter what you call him, he still won't come!

Why are elephants poor?

Because they work for peanuts.

What game do you NOT want to play with an elephant?

Squash!

Why did the boy stand behind the horse?

He thought he might get a kick out of it.

What's a good name for a horse?

Winnie.

What do you call a camel without humps?
Humphrey.

What does it mean if you find a horseshoe in the road?

It means that there's some poor horse out there walking around in its socks.

When is a black dog not a black dog?

When it's a greyhound.

What do you call a horse with seven legs?

A seven-legged horse.

What kind of fish chews bubblegum?
The blowfish.

If fruit comes from a fruit tree, where does turkey come from?

A poul-tree!

What happened when the turkey got into a fight?

He got the stuffing knocked out of him.

What do you call it when it rains chickens and ducks?

Fowl weather!

What baby is born with whiskers?

A kitten.

How should you treat a baby goat?

Like a kid.

Why do chickens lay eggs?

Because bears don't.

What fish do knights eat?

Swordfish.

How did the frog die?

It croaked.

Who was the first to ever have a mobile home?

A turtle.

Why do dogs have fur?

If they didn't, they'd be a little bear.

What animal grows the fastest?

The kangaroo, by leaps and bounds!

Which pine has the sharpest needles?

A porcupine.

How are wolves like cards?

They belong to a pack.

How can you tell if there's an elephant in your refrigerator?

You can't close the door.

Why can you never spot a leopard?

Because they're already born that way.

What animal makes the best neighbor?

A horse!

What kind of worms read?
Bookworms.

What do you call a fish without an eye?
Fsh.

What did the monkey say when he cut off his tail?
"It won't be long now!"

Why did King Kong climb up the side of the building?
The elevator was busted.

What do you call a snake with a winning personality?
A snake charmer.

What dogs love science?
Labs!

How do you close a letter in the ocean?

With a seal.

What's the rudest bird?

A mockingbird.

Which fish is the most affectionate?

The cuddlefish!

Why did the dog jump for joy?

Joy was holding a box of dog biscuits.

What do lazy dogs do for fun?

They chase parked cars.

How do mosquitos keep their hair in place?

With bug spray.

Why did a moth eat a firefly?

He needed a light snack.

What fish *never* stop complaining?

Carp.

What bug is the messiest?
The litterbug.

What kind of a wig can hear?

An earwig.

What's green and jumps?

A frog with hiccups.

If a rooster laid a brown egg and a white egg,
what kind of chicks would hatch?

Roosters don't lay eggs. Hens do.

What do you get when you put a
pair of glasses on Simba?
A see lion.

Two monkeys are hanging out in a tree. One jumps off, and then the other one does, too. Why?

Because monkey see, monkey do.

If a pony were president, how would they travel?

On Air Horse One.

How can you lift an elephant with one hand?

Worry about that after you've found an elephant that only has one hand.

What has 12 tails, a horn, and squeals?
A dozen pigs in a pickup truck.

What part of the turkey has the most feathers?

The outside of the turkey.

What animal turns around a few hundred times after it dies?

A chicken . . . on a rotisserie.

What's covered in hair and has eight to spare?

A cat.

What key opens a banana?

A monkey.

What has one eye, four legs, and half a rear end?

Half a lobster!

Why can't a tyrannosaurus clap?

Because it's extinct.

2
PLAYING WITH WORDS

Now, Here, This!

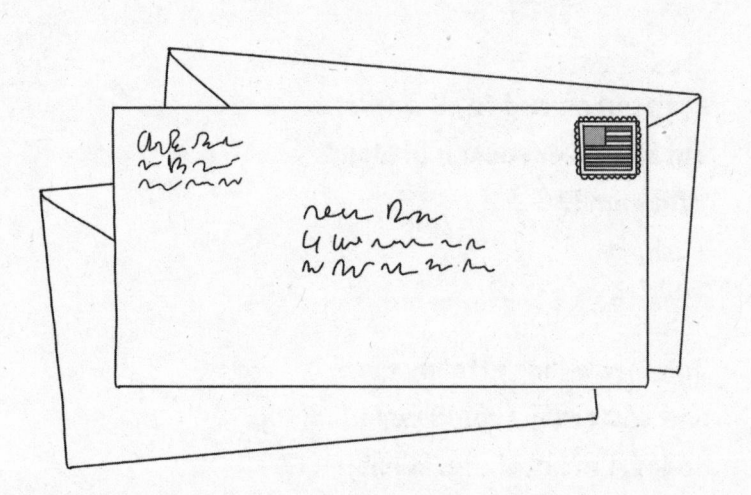

What word starts with an "e," but has just one letter?
An envelope.

I'm a five-letter word that, when typed in
ALL CAPS,
forms the same word upside down.
What am I?
SWIMS.

Spell it forward, and you do it everyday.
Spell it backward, and it's the worst thing ever.
What is it?
Live (evil).

I can put an end to all words,
but I'm never spoken of aloud.
What am I?
A period.

Tomorrow I'm certainly here,
and yesterday I could be found, too.
Today, I'm not there. What am I?
The letter "r."

What word is always pronounced wrong?
"Wrong."

What always comes at the beginning of parades?
The letter "p"!

What word becomes shorter when you add two letters to it?

Short—it becomes "shorter."

What can you break just by saying it?

Silence.

Name a dirty word.

Dirt!

What four letters scare a burglar?
O-I-C-U.

What's the world's longest word?

Rubber—it stretches!

Why is "B" the hottest letter?

Because it makes "oil" "boil."

What's the longest word in the dictionary?

Smiles: There's a mile between each "s"!

What word is both short and long?

Abbreviation.

What's longer than forever?

Any word that's eight letters or more.

What is the coolest letter in the alphabet?
"B." It's always surrounded by A/C.

What's the only letter in a golfer's alphabet?
"T"!

Spell the word "we" with two letters, but without using "w" or "e."
"U" and "I."

Can you spell "eighty" with just to letters?
A-T.

How do you spell "pound" with two letters?
L-B.

Which letter is the most explosive?
"N." It's in the middle of TNT.

If you call me right, you will be wrong.
If you call me wrong, you will
be right.
What am I?
The word "wrong."

What's a 10-letter word that starts
with gas?
Automobile!

With four As and one B, what's the smartest state?
Alabama.

**What comes once in a minute,
twice in a moment,
but never in a thousand years?**
The letter "m."

When does Christmas come before Thanksgiving?
In the dictionary.

How can you make seven even?
Remove the letter "s."

What letter flies and stings?
"B"!

There are two of me in a corner, one in a room, and none in a house.
What am I?
The letter "r."

How many letters are there in the alphabet?
Eleven: Three in "the" plus eight in "alphabet."

How do you make your ma mad?
Get a D!

What starts with a "p,"
ends with an "e,"
and has thousands of letters in it?
The post office.

What do you find in the middle of nowhere?
The letter "h"!

What's never out of sight?
The letter "s."

If the alphabet goes from A to Z,
what goes from Z to A?
"Zebra."

Which letter is small, green, and round?

"P."

How do you make the number one disappear?

Add the letter "g" and it's gone.

Which letter of the alphabet has the most water?

The "c."

What starts with a "t," ends with a "t,"
and is filled with "t"?
Teapot.

What's the shortest month?

May. (It's only three letters.)

What's the exact middle of America?

The letter "r."

What state is the loudest?

IlliNOISE.

How do make a witch itch?
Take off the "w."

When is a teacher also your friend?

When it's a princi-PAL.

"Railroad crossing without any cars."
Can you spell that without using the letter "r"?

T-H-A-T.

What question must always be answered "Yes"?

"How do you spell 'yes'?"

The turtle took two trips to Texas to teach Tommy to tie his tie. How many times does "t" appear in that? There are two in "that."

Can you spell "enemy" with three letters?
F-O-E.

If Washington's wife's washerwomen went to Washington,
and his own washerwoman stayed home,
how many "W"s are there in all?
There are no "W"s in "all."

What part of Canada is in Brazil?
The "A."

What's the longest punctuation mark?

The 100-yard dash.

What comes after "L"?

"Bow."

Name two days starting with T, but not Tuesday and Thursday.

Today and tomorrow.

Where will you always find happiness?
In the dictionary.

What's the center of gravity?

"V."

**What will you always find at the end of
a road?**

O-A-D.

What's the capital of Massachusetts?

"M."

What will you find at the end of a rainbow?
"W."

What's the one thing between the earth and sky?

"And."

Does England have a Fourth of July?

Yeah, it's right after the Third of July.

If you remove some of me, you'll surely make trouble. What am I?

Troublesome.

Forward, I'm heavy. Backwards, I'm not. What am I?

A ton. (It's "not" backward.)

What goes "mooz-mooz"?
A backwards race car.

What will you find in every riddle?

Iddle.

I am the shortest complete sentence in the English language.
I am right in front of you.
What am I?

I am "I am."

3
IT'S ONLY NATURAL

Because Life Is Funny

What's the only kind of lion that
doesn't hunt for prey?
A dandelion.

What type of jacket should you never put on?

A yellow jacket.

While not too bright, I reflect some light.
You cannot see me if it isn't the night.
What am I?

The moon.

It never stops running but has no legs.
It screams but has no voice.
It always falls down but never gets up.
What is it?

A waterfall.

When will water stop running down hill?

When it reaches the bottom.

What falls . . . but never breaks?

Nightfall.

When is a bright idea just like a clock?

When it strikes one.

What's the difference between the North Pole and the South Pole?

All the difference in the world!

When does it rain pennies and nickels?
When there's change in the weather.

Why are trees in winter like annoying houseguests?

Because it's a long time before they leave.

What can you not burn in fire, nor drown in water?

Ice.

I'm a sharp blade, but all I can cut is the wind.
What am I?

A blade of grass.

What's the only way a leopard could change its spots?
By moving from one spot to another!

They're dark and on the run, and they'd be none if it weren't for the sun.
What are they?
Shadows.

What lives if it eats but dies if it drinks?
Fire.

Before Mount Everest was discovered,
what was the highest mountain on Earth?
Still Mount Everest—
nobody knew it was the highest mountain on Earth yet.

Which is the oldest tree?
The elder.

It runs, but doesn't walk.
It has a mouth but doesn't talk.
What is it?

A river.

How can you drop a raw egg
onto a concrete floor without cracking it?

However you like—
an egg is way too small to crack a concrete floor!

What can answer in any language?

An echo.

It's light as a feather, and yet nobody can hold it for more than a minute or two. What is it?
Breath.

What constantly falls down but never gets hurt?

The rain.

Who eats a lot of iron but never gets sick?

Rust.

What are the clumsiest things in space?

Falling stars.

**I'm noisy but invisible,
but my companion is very bright but makes no noise.
What are we?**

Thunder and lightning.

What kind of tree can you carry in your hand?
A palm.

I keep a lot of things for you
but you can't physically remove any of those things.
What am I?
Your mind.

What can speak without a mouth?
An echo.

When is the best time to use a trampoline?
The spring!

Why did the gardener plant light bulbs?
She wanted to grow a power plant.

What room has no doors or windows?
A mushroom.

What's the sleepiest mountain in the world?

Mount Everest.

In what state is Lake Michigan?

A liquid state.

What's the difference between lightning and electricity?

There's no such thing as a lightning bill.

How do you fix a short circuit?

Make it longer.

When can a man walk on water?
When the water freezes over.

What has dozens of limbs but can't walk?

A tree.

How can a net hold water?

When it's in the form of ice cubes.

What has one eye and makes it rain?

A hurricane.

**No matter how cold you get,
never build a fire in a kayak!**

After all, you can't have your kayak, and heat it too.

How do you know when the moon is broke?
When it's on its last quarter.

What is dark but made by light?

A shadow.

What's brown and dirty?

Dirt.

Why is the moon like a dollar?

It has four quarters.

**If you trip on a ladder,
what do you fall against?**

Your will.

How do you fix a broken berry?
With a berry patch.

What's the difference between a big hill and a big pill?
One is hard to get up, and the other is hard to get down.

What's the healthiest water you can drink?
Well water.

What kind of bulbs don't require water or planting?
Light bulbs.

What goes through water but doesn't get wet?
A light beam.

How can you tell that the sun is very educated?
It has a million degrees.

What flower can you find on every face?

Tulips.

What tree would you find in a kitchen?

A pantry.

What kind of water can't you freeze?

Hot water.

Why did the geologist quit?

Because rocks were too hard.

What color is rain?
Watercolor.

Is the beach a positive place?
Shore!

What kind of electricity do they use in the national capitol?
D.C.!

What happens when you get a huge electric bill?
It's shocking!

What kind of garden grows children?
A kindergarden.

Most animals need me *and* you can find me in a book. What am I?

A spine.

It's cold at the top and warmer down below. What am I?

A mountain.

How do you make a waterfall?

Pour a glass of water . . . and then tip it over.

What may go up and down but never moves?

The temperature.

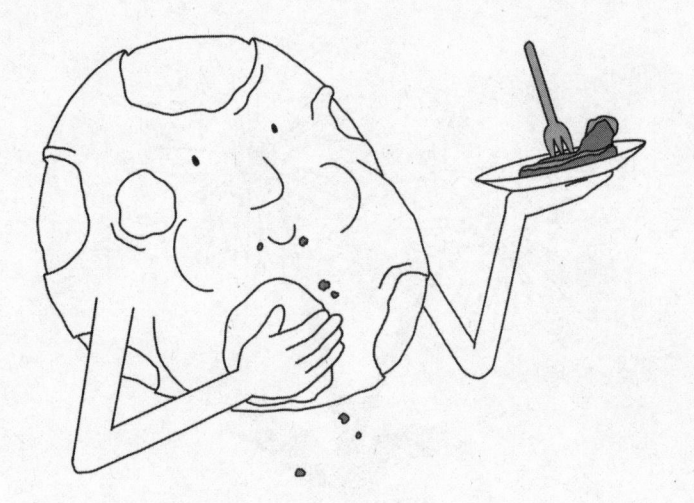

When is the moon the heaviest?
When it's full.

The more you have of it, the less you'll see.
What is it?
Darkness.

What can you make that you can't see?
Noise.

They come out at night without being called,
and are lost in the day without being stolen.
What are they?
Stars.

I have a yellow face, white hair, and a green body.
What am I?
A daisy.

What's hard as a rock but melts in hot water?

An ice cube.

What has lots of ears but cannot hear?

A field of corn.

What has a bark and lives but isn't a dog?

A tree.

What travels faster, hot or cold?

Cold. Have you ever caught a hot?

What can run but can't walk?
Water.

What happens if you throw a yellow rock into the Red Sea?
It gets wet.

Can you start a fire with one stick?
Yes, if the stick is a match.

What's made of wood but can't be sawed?
Sawdust.

If you're swimming in the Pacific Ocean and an alligator attacks, what should you do?
Don't worry about it—there are no alligators in the ocean.

Why won't a mountain catch a cold?
Because it has a snow cap.

I'm always in the sky, off in the distance,
but if you get closer I always move away.
What am I?
The horizon.

One gives birth to the other and she,
in turn, gives birth to the first.
Who are these characters?
Day and night.

What flies when it's born and lies when it's alive and disappears when it dies? A snowflake.

You heard me speak, and then again. And then I drift away until you call me once more. What am I?

An echo.

I have many rings and get a new one each year, but they aren't worth much. What am I?

A tree.

I can be used to build castles,
but I crumble in your hands. What am I?
Sand.

I can fill a room but don't take up any space.
What am I?
Light.

I'm lighter than my materials.
You can see just a part of me.
What am I?
An iceberg.

I can't be stolen, but I can be given out.
Everyone has me, and please share me.
What am I?
Knowledge.

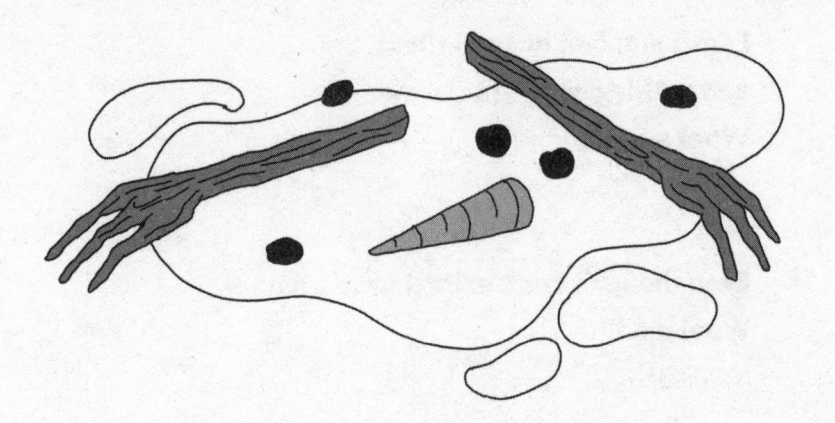

What do you call a summer snowman?
A puddle.

I'm invisible and weigh nothing, and if you put me in a
barrel, it will become lighter.
What am I?
A hole.

I can fly, and you'll miss me when I'm gone.
What am I?
Time.

I drape the hills in white and don't swallow
(but I do bite).
What am I?
Frost.

**I am a number, but countless,
and nothing compares to me.
What am I?**

Infinity.

**Even though I don't exist, I have a name.
What am I?**

Nothing!

**I have seven colors, but no gold.
What am I?**

A rainbow.

Where would you find an ocean with no water?
On a globe.

I'm as old as the earth but every month I'm new.
What am I?
The moon.

I'm in the middle of water but I'm not an island.
What am I?
Water!

What's brown and sticky?
A stick.

The colder it gets, I shed my clothes. What am I?
A tree.

How do we know the ocean is friendly?
All the waves!

I can speak every language,
even though I never learned any of them.
What am I?
An echo.

I'm a bow that cannot be tied.
What am I?
A rainbow.

I'm light as air, but if you hold me, I'll break.
What am I?
A bubble.

What's the worst thing about snow boots?
They melt.

Andrea was born on Christmas but her birthday is in the summer.
How?
She lives in Australia.

What breaks but never falls?
Daybreak.

It lives in winter, dies in summer, and grows with its roots on top?
What is it?
An icicle.

How many apples grow on a tree?
All of them.

Where would you find the English channel if you don't have a TV?
On a map.

What never gets any wetter, no matter how much it rains?
The ocean!

Everyone has me but no one can lose me. What am I?
A shadow.

What types of stones do you never find in the ocean?
Dry ones.

You go into the woods to get it, sit down to find it,
and bring it home because you can't find it.
What is it?
A splinter.

I'm a field that goes on forever,
but I have no grass and you can't walk across me.
What am I?
The ocean.

I can bring a smile to your face, or a tear in your eye.
I can make you feel angry, too.
But you can never see me nor touch me.
What am I?

A memory.

What unit of time weighs the least?

A light year.

Where in the world does the wind blow south . . . then suddenly north?

The South Pole.

I don't eat food, but I enjoy a light meal. What am I?
A plant (which stays alive with photosynthesis).

I fly, but have no wings.
I cry without eyes.
What am I?
A cloud.

What's clear as day or murky as night,
and either way you need it to be alright?
Water.

What class can you get an A in
but still wind up with a C?
Oceanography. (C = sea!)

What sneaks behind you in the day,
and disappears in the night?
Your shadow.

4
SPORTS AND LEISURE

It's All in the Game (If You're Game)

What would you get if a pig played football?
A swinebacker.

Say you're running a race.
You pass the person in second place.
Now what place are you in?
Second place.
You took over the spot, but you're yet to pass the first-place runner.

A man pushes his car along the road, and comes to a hotel.
He shouts, "I'm bankrupt!" Why?
He's playing Monopoly.

A girl learning to drive went down a one-way street the wrong way,
and yet she didn't break the law. Why?
She was walking.

Ten people hang out on a boat.
There's nobody below deck,
but there's not a single person in sight.
How is this possible?
Everyone is married.

A man buys a new car.
He pays $10,000 and walks away without paying a dime. How?
He didn't pay a dime—he paid $10,000.

What can you serve, but you never want to eat?
A volleyball.

**A whole family forgot their umbrella for their walk,
but nobody got wet.
How?**

It wasn't raining!

**A girl threw a ball 20 feet away.
It came back immediately at the same speed.
Nobody touched it.
It didn't hit any object.
How did she do it?**

She threw it directly up into the air.

There's a kid who can tell the exact score before every soccer game.
What's his secret?
The score before every soccer game is always 0-0.

If an electric car travels south, which way does the exhaust blow?
There isn't any smoke—it's an electric car.

How many books can you put into an empty backpack?
One. After that it's not empty.

What's the tallest building in town?
A library—it's got thousands of stories!

What has 60 feet and sings?
A school choir.

What kind of drawings do New York baseball players make?
Yankee doodles.

What happened when the coach tied the soccer team's shoelaces together? They had a field trip!

How do joggers bathe?
In running water.

If your watch breaks, why can't you play sports?

You no longer have the time.

Why did the batter not run when he got a hit?

Because he was already home.

How does one eliminate a fear of hurdles?

Get over it!

In what sport do you sit down while going up,
and stand up while going down?
Skiing.

What has 18 legs and catches flies?

A baseball team.

Why did St. Patrick drive all the snakes out of Ireland?

He couldn't afford plane fare for all of them.

Why would authors make weird animals?

Because tales come out of their heads!

Why are Saturday and Sunday the strongest of days?
Because all the other ones are weak-days.

Which football team is the biggest?
The Giants.

What's the quietest sport?
Bowling—you can hear a pin drop.

What sport is the loudest?
Tennis—they raise a racket!

What medical condition makes you better at sports?
Athlete's foot.

What animal is good at baseball?
A bat.

If a regular man shops at a market,
where does Superman shop?

A market as well.

What do you call a dad from the south?

A southpaw.

A boy and a dog went down the street.
The boy ran, yet walked.
What was the dog's name?

Yet.

Who are the only non-royals
who can ride in a carriage?
Babies!

What guy should you get to change your tire?

Jack!

What's the best day to go to the beach?

Sunday.

Why did the kids roll down the hill?

They slipped.

Why did the other kids roll down the hill?

It beats walking.

Did you hear about the actor who fell
through the theater's floor?
It was just a stage he was going through.

I'm scary but sweet in the end.
What am I?
Halloween.

What does the Big Bad Wolf eat at a restaurant?
The waiter.

A football team plays in a domed stadium
but didn't play on the day it rained.
Why?
It was summer, when there is no football.

What sport do insects love?
Cricket!

What basketball star can jump higher than a house?

All of them—houses don't jump.

Should you play baseball on an empty stomach?

No, you should play on a baseball diamond.

What's the largest diamond in the world?

A baseball diamond.

What's a good nickname for someone who put her right hand into a lion's mouth?
Lefty.

What runs around a football field but doesn't move?

The boundary.

Two baseball teams played.
The final score was 3-1,
although no man got a hit.
How is that?

The teams were all-female teams.

What people travel the most?
Romans.

Two girls play five games of checkers,
and each wins the same number of games.
How did that happen?
They played against different people.

Who makes moves while remaining seated?
A chess player.

I work when I play and play when I work.
What am I?
A musician.

What kind of star wears sunglasses?
A rock star.

I am a ring, but square.
What am I?
A boxing ring.

What does Popeye put in his car?
Olive Oyl.

This got stolen in a stadium, but the crowd only
cheered.
What is it?
A base.

I like you a lot, but I 'll still only come once a year.
Who am I?
Santa.

What do hockey players and magicians have in common?
Hat tricks.

What school would you have to drop
out of to graduate?
Parachute school.

When is the best time for Santa to come down the chimney?

Anytime!

When does a car become not-a-car?

When it turns into a parking space.

A man was driving a black truck, with his lights off.
The moon wasn't out.
A lady wearing all black crossed the street safely.
How did the man in the truck see her?

It was in the daytime.

Which baseball player has the biggest head?
The one who wears the biggest hat!

A man enters a room in Chicago but exits it in San Francisco.

How is it possible?

The man is an airplane pilot.

What takes place on a court with a judge but no lawyers?

Tennis.

A man drives from San Francisco to Honolulu without using a drop of gasoline.

How does he do this?

He uses a sailboat.

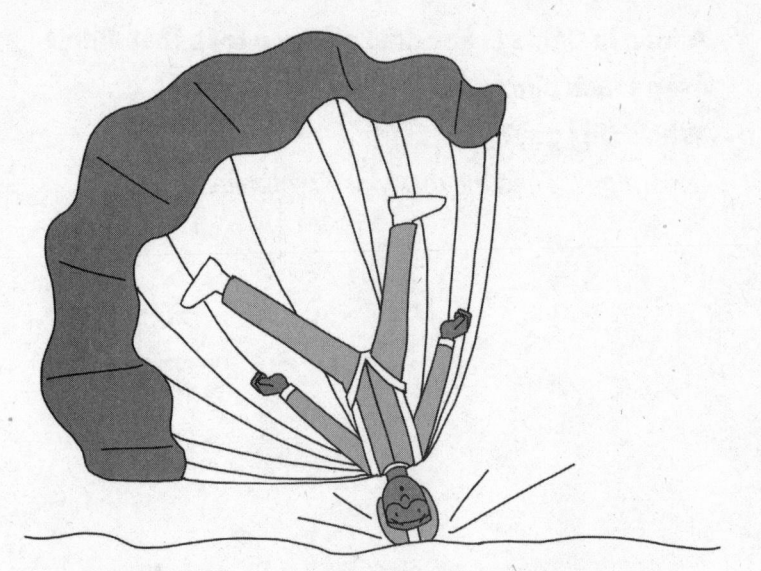

What's the hardest part about skydiving?
The ground.

Two men played five sets of tennis together and each won three sets. How did they do that?

They were partners playing doubles.

A man walks all the way around the world without getting wet. How?

He walked around a big boat that sailed all over the globe.

A man in tights is knocked out by a rock that didn't even touch him.
Who's this guy?

Superman . . . and the rock was Kryptonite.

5
THE OBJECT IS LAUGHTER

Just Some Things to Think About

I have a name but it's not mine.
I stick out of the ground but I'm not a plant.
What am I?
A tombstone.

I have no eyes of my own,
but I can see far away.
What am I?
Binoculars.

I don't live up to my name,
because you're the one who looks at me.
What am I?
A wristwatch.

You have to use me to get to another space,
and yet I always remain in place.
What am I?
A doorknob.

What keeps you in place as you travel,
that wraps around you as it unravels?
A seatbelt.

What do all hands touch,
but it never loses its green color?
Money.

If you can pick this one, it didn't do its job.
What is it?
A lock.

What's taken from a mine,
closed in a wooden case,
and is only released a little at a time . . . if
pressed?
Pencil lead.

I look like a mirror but show you the world.
I can be used for fun or education.
What am I?
A television.

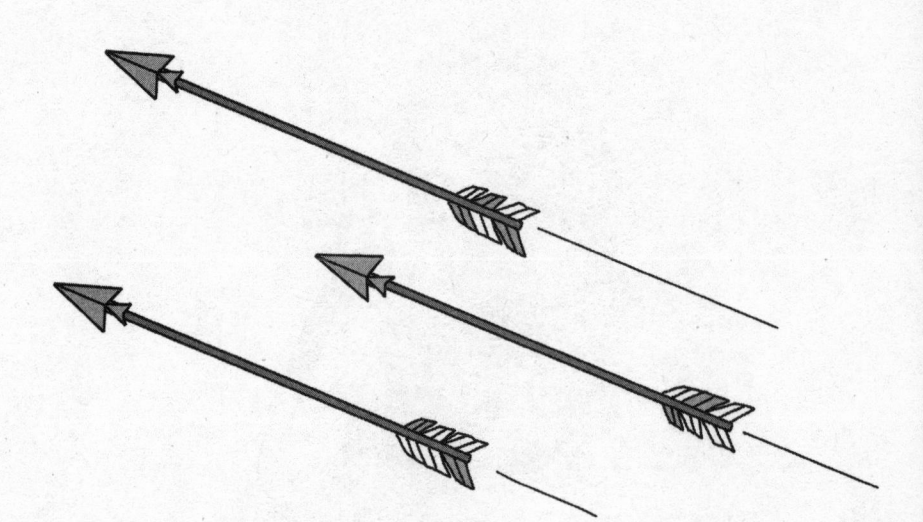

What has a head and body and flies with feathers...
but how far depends on you?
An arrow.

I have a few points, and I'll use those to help you eat. What am I?

A fork.

I go into the water red and I come out black. What am I?

A red-hot iron.

What goes up and down the stairs without moving?

Carpet.

I sit on a bridge and people see the world through me even though I make things a little dark. What am I?
Sunglasses.

Drop me and the world will shatter.
Look for me when you empty your bladder.
What am I?
A bathroom mirror.

I fasten to walk, and unfasten to stop.
What am I?
Sandals.

I brighten your day but stay in the shade.
What am I?
A lamp.

I take off clothes when you put on your clothes.
I put on my clothes when you take off *your*
clothes.
What am I?
A clothes hanger.

What snaps at a happy moment?
A camera.

I have numbers on my face but no mouth or nose.
What am I?
A clock.

I have no voice, but I can teach you all there is to know. I'm not a door, but I have a spine. What am I?
A book.

What's big and yellow and comes in the morning to brighten Mom's day?

The school bus.

I'm hard as a rock, yet can also be light as paper. Poor people need me, rich people have me. What am I?

Money.

I live on a busy street, and you can stay for an hour or two, so long as you pay rent. What am I?

A parking meter.

Many say I'm their favorite place,
but no one remembers their stay.
You love to arrive but hate to
leave.
What am I?
A bed.

Stick your fingers in my eyes,
I'll open my mouth wide.
What am I?
A pair of scissors.

I come in different colors and shapes.
Some parts are curvy, some
straight.
There's only one right place for each
of my many parts.
What am I?
A jigsaw puzzle.

He who invented it doesn't want it.
He who bought it doesn't need it.
He who needs it doesn't know it.
What is it?
A coffin.

I'm very simple, but powerful enough that people all the world go where I point. What am I?
A compass.

I look like a city wall from far away, but a row of houses up close.
And yet it all stays in a line as it travels thousands of miles.
What is it?
A train.

I give directions to others but none to myself.
I can tell you your way around, and without me you'd get lost.
What am I?
A street sign.

The more you work, the more I can eat.

Keep me full, I'll keep things clean.

What am I?

A pencil sharpener.

I go up, and then I go down. And then I do it again.
And again. It's fun! What am I?
A see-saw.

Take whatever you want out of me for free.

Return what you don't want and I'll keep it safe until

you're ready for it.

What am I?

A closet.

What has feet on the inside but never on the outside?
Shoes.

What has a head . . . but can't think . . . but *can* drive?
A hammer.

What do you do if you swallow a pen?
Use a pencil.

What do you call a boomerang that doesn't return?
A stick.

How do you put a stick on the floor so nobody can jump over it?
Put it against a wall.

I'm sharp but I have no brain.
I can do your homework for you, though.
What am I?
A pencil.

What kind of bed can you have no "accidents" in but will always be wet?
A waterbed.

It has no top or bottom but holds bones, blood, and flesh all at once. What am I?
A ring.

I say *chew-chew*, but I don't care if you eat. What am I?

A train.

What runs but never moves?

A refrigerator.

What part of a car is always exhausted?

The tail pipe.

Why is a lost object always in the last place you look?

Because if you found it, why would you keep looking?

How can you hold the whole world in your hands?
With a globe.

How can you double your money in the bathroom?
Put it in front of the mirror.

What can you open when its keys are left inside?
A piano.

**I have a neck but no head, two arms but no hands.
What am I?**
A shirt.

**I'm full of problems, but I like it that way. It's my job.
What am I?**
A math book.

Where was the Declaration of Independence signed?

At the bottom.

What goes through every town in the country but never moves?

Roads.

What's something you don't want to see on a ship?

A sink!

What's the best way to get straight As?

Use a ruler.

What's placed on a table and cut, but not eaten?
A deck of cards.

What case is not a case?

A staircase.

It has an eye for sewing but cannot see.
What is it?

A needle.

You can tickle me, but I'll never laugh.
What am I?

A piano keyboard.

Why was the toilet tired?
It had been running all day.

I look like you, but I'm frozen forever. What am I?

A photograph.

What object in the bathroom weighs the most?

The scale.

What's the difference between a shiny dime and a dirty quarter?

Fifteen cents.

Why shouldn't you clean the toilet with a smile?

A brush is far more effective.

What do computers and crash test dummies have in common?

They both crash a lot.

I help engines to turn and I also keep your pants up. What am I?

A belt.

What do you get when you cross a piece of paper with a pair of scissors?

Confetti.

I sing when asked, and I always take my bow.
What am I?
A violin.

What band never plays music?

A rubber band.

How can you instantly double your money?

Fold it in half.

What phone never rings?

A saxophone.

I tie two together but touch just one of them.
What am I?

A wedding ring.

I smell like blue paint, pour like green paint, and look like a red truck.
What am I?
Red paint!

I have 13 hearts but no body and no soul.
What am I?
A deck of cards.

I am the only thing higher than a King or queen.
What am I?
A crown.

Everyone needs me and wants me, but everyone uses me.
What am I?
Money.

I can speak, though my tongue is metal.
What am I?
A bell.

I don't leave my tracks, because they come before me.
What am I?
A train.

Why didn't the girl take the bus home?
Because she couldn't fit it in her backpack.

Every night you tell me to do my job and the next morning I do,
and you hate me for it.
What am I?
An alarm clock.

Take me for a spin and I'll make you cool.
What am I?
A fan.

What keeps its job after it's been fired?
A rocket.

I open to close but I close to open.
What am I?

A drawbridge.

It turns into a different story.
What is it?

A spiral staircase.

I'll take what you get and give it away with a wave of
my flag.
What am I?

A mailbox.

What should you give to the person who has everything?

Medicine.

Two wrongs don't make a right, but what do two rights make?

The first airplane.

Draw, fire, or fill me. I'm empty. What am I?

A blank.

Should you file your nails?
No, you can just throw them away.

A boy fell off a 25-foot-tall ladder but didn't get hurt. Why not?

He fell off the bottom step of the ladder.

What has a thumb and four fingers but doesn't live?

A glove.

What paper is the itchiest?

Scratch paper.

I have two legs, but they only touch the ground when I'm not moving. What am I?

A wheelbarrow.

Back and forth all day long . . . until I help the little ones fall asleep. What am I?

A rocking chair.

What do you throw out when you want to use it, but take it in when you *don't* want to use it?

An anchor.

What can go up a chimney down, but can't go down a chimney up?

An umbrella.

What kind of coat can you only put on when it's wet?
A coat of paint.

What stays where it is when it goes off?

An alarm clock.

What can enter a house through only a keyhole?

A key.

I let you glimpse other worlds, but you can't enter me.
You can see into me, but I can't see you.
What am I?

A TV.

I twist and turn and leave a loop.
What am I?
A shoelace.

My teeth are sharp but I have no mouth.
What am I?
A saw.

What does a box say when you seal it?
Nothing. It just shuts up.

What kind of table doesn't have legs?
A multiplication table.

What kind of watch should you use if you
don't like to have time on your hands?
A pocket watch.

What is full of lead but still extremely light?

A pencil.

Why did the writer put a flashlight in her mouth?

She was looking for an inside story.

Why is an old car like a baby?

They both have a rattle.

How is a wig like a secret?
You keep it under your hat.

What's shaped like a box, has no feet, and constantly moves?

An elevator.

What kind of eye gets hit the most?

A bullseye.

If you don't feel well, what do you have?

A pair of gloves on your hands.

How do you send a letter to a boy?

With a mailbox.

What has 50 heads and 50 tails?

50 quarters.

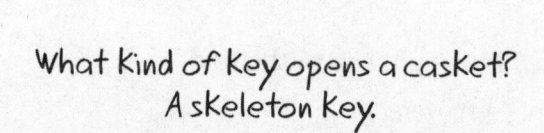

What kind of key opens a casket?
A skeleton key.

Can you trust a mummy with your secret?

Yes—they keep things under wraps.

Is paper any good?

No, it's tearable.

What wears shoes but has no feet?

A sidewalk.

How is a fancy fabric like a chair?

It's satin.

What's pointed in one direction but headed the other?

A pin.

What car drives over water?

Any car, if it uses a bridge.

Why should you build a house on flat land?

Because it's flat.

Where do you buy blue pants?

At the blue pants store.

What did the quilt say to the bed?

"I've got you covered!"

Why did the girl sit on a clock?
She needed to be on time!

Did you hear about the woman who fell into the upholstery machine?

It's fine now. She's fully recovered.

What do lawyers wear to court?

Lawsuits.

What pool can't you swim in?

A carpool.

What kind of umbrella does the president carry on a rainy day?

A wet one.

What's always behind the times?

The back of a clock.

What happens when you unplug a freezer?

It loses its cool.

Why are wallets so loud?
Because money talks.

When should you charge a battery?

When you don't have any cash to buy it.

When do cars get flat tires?

When there's a fork in the road.

What's the easiest way to make a coat last?

Make the pants first.

How does a bed grow longer?

When someone sleeps in it, it adds two feet.

What room is the bounciest?

A ballroom.

Where do fish keep their money?

In riverbanks.

Where do polar bears keep their money?

In snowbanks.

What kind of fence goes on strike?

A picket fence.

What kind of socks would you find in your yard?

Hose.

How do you make some cold hard cash?

Put it in the freezer.

Why should you never tell secrets around a clock?

Because time will tell!

What driver works without a license?

A screwdriver.

Where do farmers keep their money?
In piggy banks.

What's the best key to have?

Lucky.

What coat has the most sleeves?

A coat of arms.

What's holes tied to holes but is as strong as iron?

A chain.

What house weighs the least?

A lighthouse.

How do you shorten a bed?

Don't sleep long!

How can you make your fortune larger?

Put it under a magnifying glass.

What motive inspired the invention of the railroad?

The locomotive.

How can you avoid wrinkles?

Don't sleep in your clothes!

Why don't carpenters think stone exists?

Because they never saw it.

What sits lower with two heads then it does with only one?

A pillow.

What has a ring but no finger?

A phone.

What shoes should a spy wear?

Sneakers.

What shoes does a lazy guy wear?

Loafers.

I am made of paper, but I don't tell stories and you throw me away immediately. What am I?

Toilet paper.

How do you fix a broken primate?
With a monkey wrench.

What walks all day on its head?
A nail in a horseshoe.

What turns everything around, but doesn't move?
A mirror.

What got stolen in the music store robbery?
The lute!

Why do people wear shamrocks on St. Patrick's Day?
The real rocks are too heavy.

Why is it hard to look for a missing watch?
Because how can you find the time?

What kind of pliers are used in math?
Multipliers!

Why did the camper throw away her sleeping bag?
She couldn't wake it up.

How did Washington cross the Delaware?
In a boat.

What dish would you never eat from?
A satellite dish.

What lives off itself and dies when it's eaten itself?
A candle.

How do you find a train?

Just follow its tracks.

What has shoulders but no arms?

A highway.

Why did the teenager sleep in the fridge?

Because she was cool.

Why were the corduroy pillows in the news?

They were making headlines!

Why do kids wear heavy coats in the winter?

Because it's cold outside.

What's yellow and you can't drink?

A school bus.

What goes out even when it stays put?

A candle.

What phones work best in school?

Smartphones.

When is a green book not a green book?

When it's read.

Which school supply is king of the classroom?

The ruler.

Who doesn't ask questions but needs to be answered?

A telephone.

I don't live, but I can (and will) die.
What am I?

A battery.

What's taken before you even see it?

Your photograph.

What makes music on your hair?
A headband.

What has a neck but no head?
A bottle.

I have keys but no locks.
Space, but no room.
What am I?
A computer keyboard.

What has a head, a foot, and four legs?
A bed.

What hard rock group has four dudes but none of them play an instrument?
Mount Rushmore.

What has four legs but never runs?
A chair.

The more you take from me, the bigger I get. What am I?
A hole.

What goes up and down but never moves?
Stairs.

What has four wheels and flies?
A garbage truck.

What has cities, towns, and streets but no people?
A map.

A car takes a turn but one tire doesn't move. Which one?
The spare.

I point up for brightness and point down for darkness. What am I?
A light switch.

I have three eyes, and when I open the red one you'd better stop.
What am I?
A traffic light.

A king, queen, and twins lay in a room, but no people are present.
What's going on?
They're beds.

What has a tongue but can't talk, but gets around without walking?
A shoe.

Where do books sleep?
Under the covers.

If you use this for its purpose, its head will turn from red to black.
What is it?
A matchstick.

What's more useful if it's broken?
An egg.

What has hands but won't clap?
A clock.

You can drop me from the tallest building, and I'll survive.
Drop me in water? I die.
What am I?
Paper.

You go camping and your cabin has a wood stove, a gas stove, and a coal stove . . . but only one match.
Which do you light first?
The match!

What can travel all over the world but stays in the corner?
A postage stamp.

What runs around the whole yard without moving?

A fence.

I may be full of holes, but I can still hold water. What am I?

A sponge.

I have six faces (but no mouth) and 21 eyes (but can't see). What am I?

A die.

I'm tall when I'm young, and short when I'm old. What am I?

A candle.

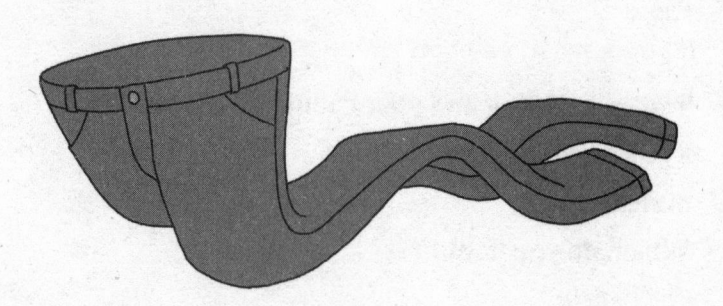

What has two legs but cannot walk?
Pants.

What has lots of keys, but can't open any door?

A piano.

What has a foot on each side and one in the middle?

A yardstick.

What has a head, a tail, no legs, and is shiny?

A quarter.

What makes a pair of shoes?

That second shoe.

What has an eye but does not see?

A needle.

If you have it, you don't keep it.
It can be large, small, any shape.
Or anything.
What is it?

A gift!

The more you dry yourself with me the more
I get wet.
What am I?

A towel.

What goes up when the rain comes down?
An umbrella.

When is a door not a door?

When it's ajar.

What has teeth but never eats?

A comb.

When may a man call his wife "honey"?

When she has a comb in her hair.

What do you purchase by the yard and wear by the foot?
Carpet!

What kind of paper can't be written on?
Sandpaper.

What has two legs but doesn't walk?
A ladder.

I'm wasteful, but I'm home to things nobody wants.
What am I?
A trash can.

What ancient, common object can allow you to walk through a wall?
A door.

You encounter me everyday, but if you're fine, I'm never quite used.
What am I?
A seat belt.

I'm not clothes, but I go all over your body.
The more you use me, the thinner I get.
What am I?
A bar of soap.

Why did the photograph go to jail?
It was framed!

I have a head, and a tail, but don't have a body.
What am I?
A coin.

Eight of these go out to protect their kind from enemies,
moving just one or two steps at a time.
What are they?
Pawns in a chess game.

6
A BODY OF HUMOR

Inside Jokes

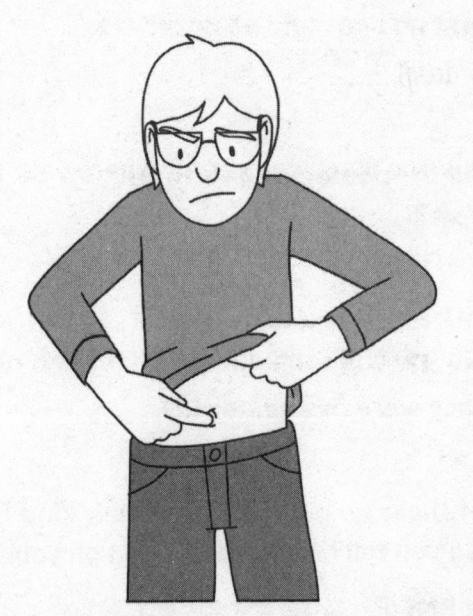

What button doesn't do anything if you press it?
A belly button.

How can people who don't have noses smell?

If they don't wear deodorant.

What's the first thing you should put in a room?

Your feet.

What's the proper length for a woman's dress?

A little above two feet.

What has no body and no nose?

Nobody nose!

Where is one place you can sit where your mom cannot sit?

Your mom's lap.

What do you call someone who has been running since they were five years old?

Tired!

How can you tell if reindeer landed on your roof on Christmas Eve?

Look for yellow icicles!

What's the very best thing to put into a pie?
Your teeth!

Say a whale swallows you.
How do you get out?
Run around as hard as you can until you're
pooped.

What's the difference between a hungry man and a
glutton?
One longs to eat and the other eats
too long.

Long or short, painted or bare, I sit near
your hands and feet. What am I?
Nails.

What definitely tastes better than it smells?

A tongue.

**What are moving left to right, right this
very minute?**

Your eyes.

What can you catch but not throw?

A cold!

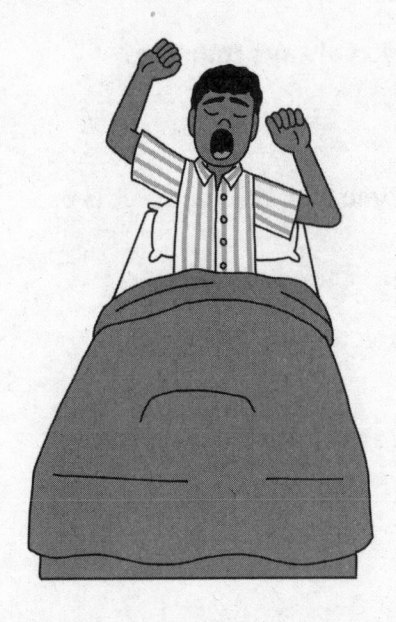

What's the first thing you do in the morning?
You wake up!

What does even the most careful person constantly overlook?

Their nose.

You can hear and use me but never touch me or see me.
What am I?

Your voice.

What can you always count on?
Your fingers.

The faster you run, the harder it is to catch me.
What am I?
Your breath.

You can use me but can't touch me.
What am I?
Your brain.

A man goes out in heavy rain with nothing to protect him from it. But his hair doesn't get wet. How? He didn't have any hair to get wet — he's bald.

You can hold me in your left hand but not in your right. What am I?

Your right hand.

I'm there when you sit, but disappear when you stand. What am I?

Your lap.

How many feet are in a yard?

It depends on how many people are standing around in it.

What can you steal from someone and they won't have you arrested?

Their heart.

I exist when you're here. Where you never were,
I'll never be. What am I?
Your reflection.

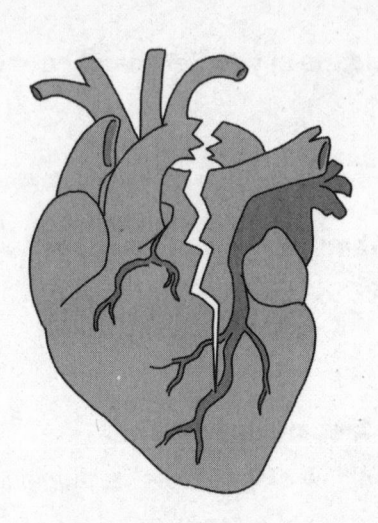

I am inside you, and I can break without being touched.
What am I?
Your heart.

What smells the most in a dump?

You!

What roof is always wet?

The roof of your mouth.

Why is the nose in the middle of the face?

Because that's the scent-er!

What do you call a ball that wears glasses?
An eyeball.

What's whinier than a teething baby?

Two teething babies.

What only has one hand?

An arm.

**I can hear everything, but I'll never say a word.
What am I?**

An ear.

What nails do carpenters avoid hitting?
Their fingernails.

What has a bottom at its top?

Your legs!

What body parts make the most music?

The organs.

What's broken if you touch your foot and it hurts, and you touch your shoulder and it hurts?

Your finger!

If you eat 3/4th of a cake, what do you get?
A stomachache.

What type of hair is the hottest?
Sideburns.

Why didn't the doctor treat the invisible patient?

He just couldn't see him.

When is the best time to go to the dentist?

At tooth-hurty.

Why didn't the gross kid flush?

It wasn't his duty.

Why did the woman run around her bed?
She needed to catch up on her sleep.

Why can't babies drive?

They have poor motor skills.

When is a booger not a booger?

When it's snot.

What would you find on the inside of an empty nose?

Fingerprints!

When do you not feel so hot?
When you have a cold.

Where was Queen Elizabeth crowned?

On her head.

What should you do if you break your leg in two places?

Don't go back to those places!

Did you pick your nose?

Nah, you were born with it.

My name might be Curly, but don't call me that if I'm heading straight. What am I?
Hair.

What gets sharper with use?

The brain.

When is a tall man also short?

When he's short on funds.

Why can't your nose be 12 inches long?
Because then it would be a foot.

How do you keep your teeth together?

With toothpaste.

What do you do if a teenager rolls his eyes at you?

Pick them up and roll them back!

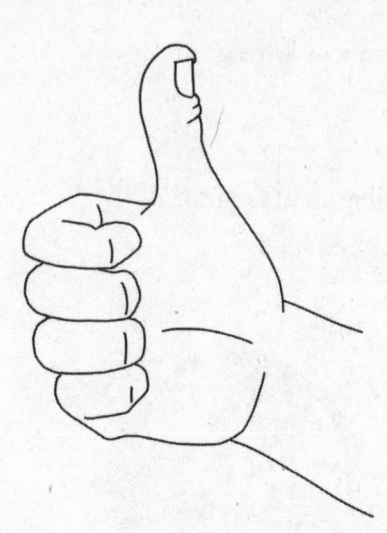

Put me to your nose to reject,
or out in the air to accept. What am I?
A thumb.

When are eyes not eyes?

When the pollen in the air makes them water.

What really makes you sweat?

Remembering you forgot to wear deodorant.

What did the worker get after he worked very, very hard?

Tired.

I'm drawn by all without a pen or pencil. What am I?
Breath.

**If a man is born in England,
raised in Canada,
came to the U.S.,
and died in Brazil, what is he?**
Dead.

**I'm part of a family of 10, but two of me make a
promise.
What am I?**
A pinky.

What can be filled with empty hands?
Mittens.

How do you eat a tent?

With your teeth.

**I have all of the knowledge that you do,
but we've never been face to face (because I don't
have a face).
What am I?**

Your brain.

Who won the "World's Best Skeleton" contest?

No body.

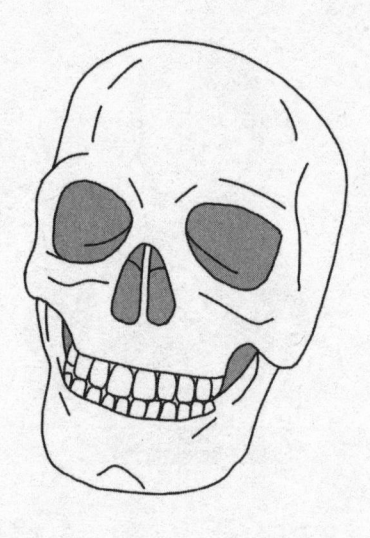

I am a head but have no face. What am I?
A skull.

What's the best cure for dandruff?

Baldness.

What happens if an icicle hits your head?

It will knock you out cold.

How did the kid feel when he hit his thumb with a hammer?

Swell!

Who is the soundest sleeper?

Someone who snores.

If you had five apples in one hand and
five bananas in the other, what do you have?
Gigantic hands!

We're twins. We're very close . . . but will
never touch.
And we always work together.
What are we?
Eyes.

Two dozen white houses stand on a red hill,
but they move together to tear things apart.
What are they?
Teeth.

I get dirty, I get clean.

People shake me or smack me against my own kind.

What am I?

Hands!

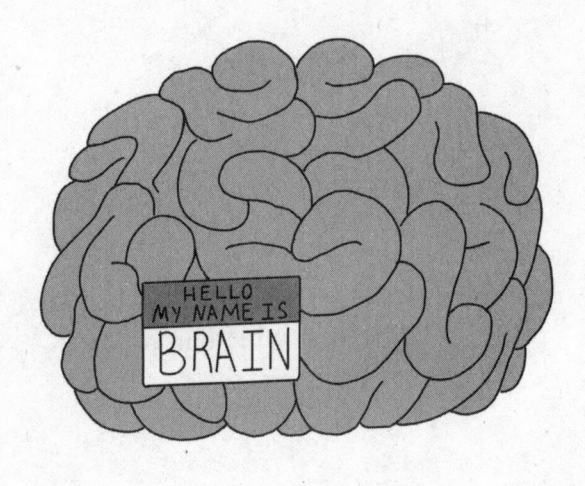

What organ named itself?
The brain.

What's the best way to keep your hat from falling off your head?

Don't put it on your head at all!

What's the last thing you take off before bed?

Your feet, off the floor.

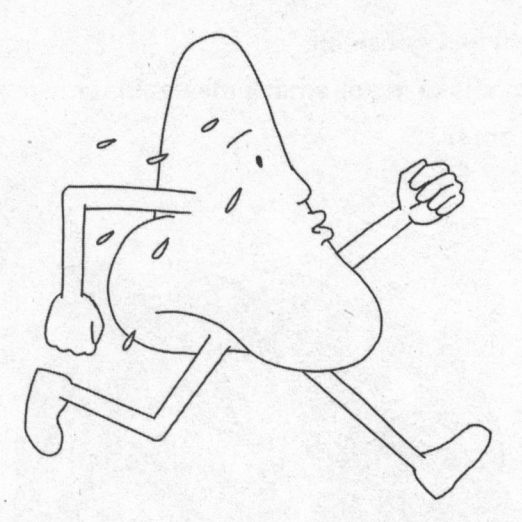

What runs the fastest in a cold?
Your nose.

What's the last thing you do at night?

You go to sleep!

I'm always with you, trailing behind.
Sometimes I'll raise a stink.
What am I?

Your rear end.

7
LET'S EAT

Tasty Treats to Test You and Best You

Sorry to be cheesy, but I'm round and also a triangle
and sometimes square. What am I?
Pizza!

You drop an egg from a second-story window and it doesn't shatter.
Why not?
It was a boiled egg.

I'm a house with two occupants, sometimes one.
Break the walls, eat the residents, then throw me away.
What am I?
A peanut.

When do you stop at green and go at red?
When eating watermelon.

What do you eat but never swallow?
Gum.

How come when you order a pizza it will never be long?
Because pizzas are round.

How do you make ground beef?
Make a cow lie down.

What looks just like half a turkey sandwich?
The other half of a turkey sandwich.

What goes in dry but comes out wet?
A teabag.

What food is the easiest to eat?

A piece of cake!

How do you make a watermelon?

Get a cantaloupe wet.

**I have beige walls that surround a white castle, and liquid gold sits in my middle.
What am I?**

An egg.

What fruit is round and orange?
A lemon on Halloween.

What makes a loud noise when changing its skin,
gets bigger but weighs less?
Popcorn.

You throw away the outside and cook the inside.
Then you eat that outside and throw away
the inside.
What is it?

Corn on the cob.

If you took two apples from three apples,
how many apples would you have?

Two apples—you took two.

When is an Irish potato not an Irish potato?
When it's a French fry.

I'm full of milk but I am not a cow.
What am I?
A milk carton.

Leftovers? I've got you covered.
What am I?
Aluminum foil.

Green means don't, red means do,
and you can't wait for me to catch up.
What am I?
A tomato.

What should you do to ensure sweet dreams?
Put candy under your pillow.

How can you tell the difference between a can of tuna and a can of cat food?

Read the label!

What cup can't hold water?

A cupcake.

If you dropped a tomato on your foot, would it hurt?

It would if it were still in the can.

How do you prevent getting a pain in the eye when you drink chocolate milk?

Take the spoon out of the glass before you drink it.

What's the opposite of a hot dog?
A chili dog.

What's the difference between a fish and a piano?

You can't tuna piano.

When is an apple not an apple?

When it's a pineapple.

How do you make a lemon drop?

Let it go!

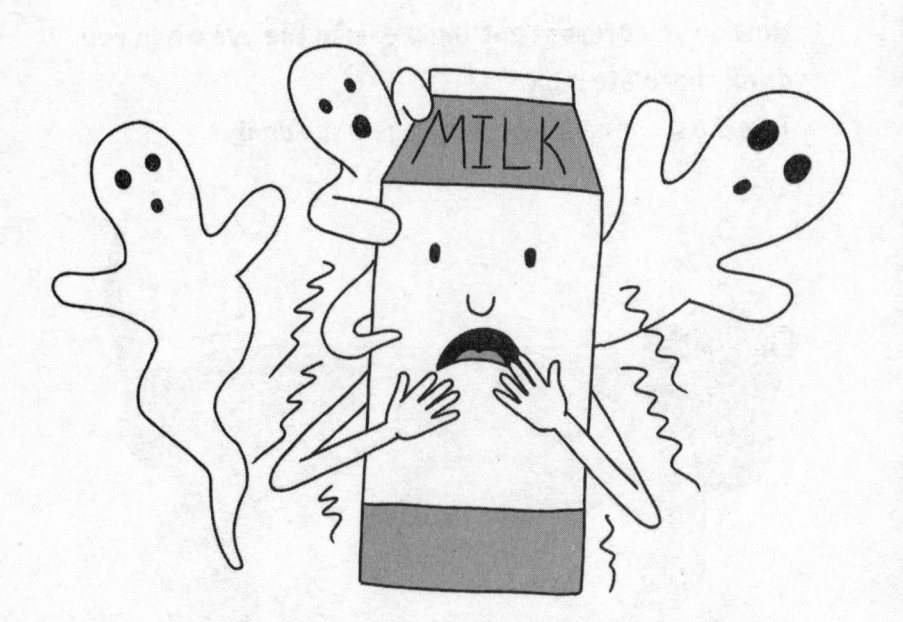

How do you make a milk shake?
Give the milk a good scare.

How do you get fat?

Fry up some bacon.

What stays hot even in a refrigerator?

Hot sauce.

What's the best way to catch a fish?

Have someone throw one at you.

I'm dressed in red and I've got a stone inside me.
What am I?
A cherry.

What beans don't grow?

Jelly beans.

When do you swallow your words?

When you eat alphabet soup.

What's the best way to eat lasagna?

Open your mouth!

How do you make a butterfly?
Throw some butter out of a window.

What has a head but no brain?

A cabbage.

How do you prevent milk from spoiling?

Leave it in the cow.

What dog never barks?

A hot dog.

I'm a great summer treat and I'm also the pits.
What am I?
A peach.

What fruit is always on the calendar?

Dates.

How do you make a banana split?

Cut it in half.

Who gets the most fed up with people?

Cannibals.

What cookie makes you rich?

Fortune cookies.

What fruits come in twos?
Pears.

Who loves cocoa?

A coconut!

What kind of cake do chickens eat?

Layer cake.

How can you be sure the dog ate your homework?

Feed it to him.

Why did the kid leave cheese by his computer?

To feed the mouse.

If cheese goes on top of a hamburger,
what comes after cheese?
Mice.

Why did the boy put a cake in the freezer?

It needed icing.

What happens if you drink food coloring?

You dye a little on the inside.

What's the hardest cake?
Marble cake.

Which is the left side of a pie?

The side not yet eaten!

What type of vest is the most delicious?

A harvest.

Where do they get tough chickens?
From hard-boiled eggs.

How do you make a hot dog stand?

Steal its stool.

What do bakers put on their beds?

Cookie sheets.

What do boxers drink?

Punch!

How do you make a banana split?

Tell it to scram.

Why is ranch never ready?
It's always dressing.

How do you make a cream puff?

Make it run a few miles.

What's the best way to eat a banana?

Without the peel.

Why are lunch trays so generous?

Because lunch is always on them.

What animal lives inside a melon?
A cantelope.

**French fries aren't from France.
Where are they from?**

Greece.

What do you call a pig that stands in the sun for too long?

Bacon!

How do you make a root beer float?

Throw the can in the tub.

When do you not have to worry
about a moose in your house?
When it's a chocolate mousse.

What nut has no shell?
A doughnut.

What comes in a brown sack,
and even though you don't know what it's in it, you'll
eat it?

Lunch!

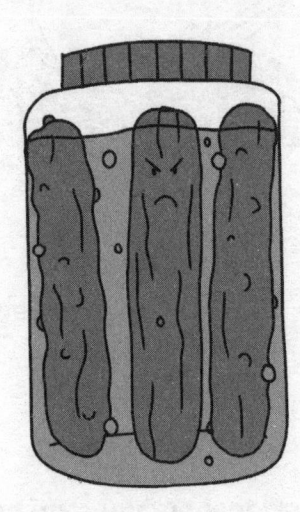

Why was the cucumber mad?
It got in a pickle.

How do make a golden soup?

With 14 carrots.

Why did the scrambled egg give up?

Because it knew when it had been beaten.

What do vegetarian chickens sit on?
Eggplants.

How do you know that potatoes are healthy?
You've never seen one at the doctor, have you?

What kind of cheese is made backwards?
Edam.

How many peas are there in a pint?
There's only one "p" in a pint.

What kind of nut costs the most?
A cashew.

What submarine can you eat?
A submarine sandwich.

Holly's smartphone fell into a big mug of coffee but didn't get wet.
How was that possible?
It was dry, ground coffee.

Two people both eat exactly half of a chocolate bar,
but one eats more than the other. How?
They each eat half of different chocolate bars.

What kind of nut has a hole and is squishy?
A doughnut.

Why couldn't the egg lend money?
It was broke.

What's a tortilla chip's favorite kind of music?
Salsa.

What do you put out for dinner but never eat?
Silverware.

What gets harder only when you put it in hot water?

An egg.

What two things can you never eat for breakfast?

Lunch and dinner.

If you remove my skin, I won't cry...but you might.
What am I?
An onion.

8
THE SILLY SECTION

Ridiculous Riddles to Really Rile

Imagine you are in a dark room full of
ghosts and goblins. How do you get out?
Stop imagining!

When you know not what I am, I'm something.
When you do know what I am, then I'm nothing.
What am I?

A riddle!

You can find me on tops of mountains,
on tall buildings,
and at the height of a winding staircase.
What am I?

Dizziness.

He lays dead, a metalized bar across his back.
The man who did it is very happy.
It's all legal. What happened?

The man had caught a mouse in a mousetrap.

You just got two holes in your new shirt!
How many holes are in it?

Six—it already had four holes (two arms, a neck, and the bottom).

What does a professional illustrator most like to draw?

Her salary.

On which side of a church is a graveyard placed?

On the outside!

Oliver is six feet tall, works in a butcher shop, and wears size 10 shoes. What does he weigh? Meat. (He works in a butcher shop!)

Who actually enjoys poor health?

A doctor.

How can a pants pocket be empty, but still have something in it?

Well, it can have a hole in it.

How many seconds are in a year?

Just twelve. January 2nd, February 2nd, March 2nd . . .

I make bridges of silver and crowns of gold. Who am I?
A dentist.

If you live in a one-story house made of redwood, what color are the stairs?

There are no stairs in a one-story house.

A man left town on Sunday, stayed a night at a hotel, and rode back to town the next day on Sunday. How did he do that?

Sunday is the name of his horse.

Why is an older one-hundred-dollar bill worth more than a new one?

Because $100 is worth more than $1.

Where do you go through one hole, and then come out through two holes at the same time? When you put on a pair of pants.

How many bricks does it take to complete a tower made entirely of bricks?

One, as the last one completes the tower.

What's the one question you can honestly never say "yes" to?

"Are you sleeping?"

How far can a dog run into the woods?

Halfway. Otherwise she'd be running out of the woods.

If a red house is made of red bricks,
and a yellow house is made of yellow bricks,
what is a greenhouse made of?
Glass.

What goes up but never comes down?
Your age.

What's easy to get into but hard to get out of?
Trouble!

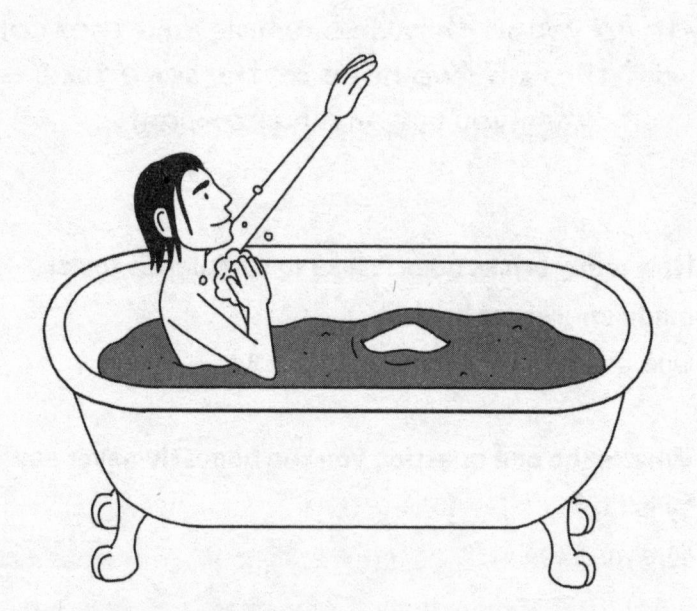

What gets dirty after washing?
Bathwater.

During what month do people sleep the least?

February, because it's the shortest month.

Brendan's mother had three children.
The first child was named May,
the second child was named June.
What was the third child's name?

Brendan.

How much dirt is there in a hole with a three-foot diameter?

There is no dirt in the hole.

How many months in the year have 28 days?

All of them.

In Massachusetts, you can't take a picture of a person with a pirate hat.
Why?

Because you need a camera to take pictures, not a pirate hat.

Two mothers and two daughters go to a pet store and buy a total of three dogs. Each female gets her own new pet. How is this possible?

They're grandmother, mother, and daughter.

Who shaves 30 times a day and can still sport a beard?
A barber.

How many sides are there to a circle?
Two—the inside and the outside.

Who earns money without working a single day?
Anybody who works nights.

Why do people build new houses?
Because you can't build old houses.

How can somebody walk for 10 days without sleeping?
If they sleep at night.

If you had 20 men build your house in two months, how long would it take 10 men to build the very same house?

No time at all, because the house was already built by the 20 men.

When the kid's jacket fell on the floor, why did it make such a loud noise?

The kid was still wearing it.

Who doesn't turn out the lights before bed?
A lighthouse keeper.

Why did the astronauts launch in separate rockets?

The needed some space.

What did the angry man say when he walked into a restaurant?

"Ow!"

What did the policeman say when he lost his car?

"Hey, where's my car?"

What does a math teacher find odd?

Numbers like 3, 5, and 9.

How do you greet a five-headed monster?
Hi, hi, hi, hi, hi!

What do a horse and an apple have in common?

Neither one is purple.

Why does the Statue of Liberty stand outside New York?

Because she can't sit down.

Who succeeded the first king of England?

The second one.

Who *didn't* invent the airplane?

The Wrong Brothers.

What do you call a pirate with two eyes and two legs?
A new pirate.

What does a clock have at every meal?

Seconds!

What do Ivan the Terrible and Winnie the Pooh have in common?

They have the same middle name: "the."

Why haven't astronauts been to Mars?

Nobody invited them.

Where won't you find any uncles?
In Aunt-Arctica.

How do you know you didn't learn much in school today?
Because you have to go back tomorrow!

What's the speediest country on Earth?
Russia.

How do you solve a riddle about frozen orange juice?
Concentrate!

What kind of criminal doesn't bathe?
A dirty crook.

What bet can you never win?

The alphabet.

If a man carrying lamps drops one, what does he become?

A lamp lighter.

Who kills but never goes to jail?

An exterminator.

How can you eat an egg without breaking a shell?

Ask someone else to break it for you.

Why are robbers so strong?
They hold people up.

Why are city people not that smart?

The population is very dense.

What's more invisible than the Invisible Man?

The Invisible Man's shadow.

Who's bigger, Mr. Bigger or his baby?

His baby. She's a little Bigger.

What kind of ears would you find on a train?

Engineers.

What bus crossed the ocean?
Columbus.

Why do firefighters wear red suspenders?
To keep their pants up.

Why do we put baby girls in pink and baby boys in blue?

Because they're too small to dress themselves.

How do we know Rome was built at night?

Because Rome wasn't built in a day.

What kind of road has the most ghosts haunting it?

A dead end!

What did Tennessee?

The same thing that Arkansas.

Why do letter carriers deliver the mail?
Because it can't deliver itself.

What doctors are always in a bad mood?

Dentists—they're often down in the mouth.

What do seven days of starvation do?

It makes one weak.

How are 2 + 2 = 5 and your left hand alike?

Neither one is right!

Why did the kid get such a small phone bill?

Because talk is cheap!

What happens after a kitten turns six months old?
It turns seven months old.

Where do walls like to meet up?

At the corner.

What time is it when a clock strikes 13?

Time to get a new clock.

Why did the man put a clock under his desk?

He had to work overtime.

Why can't we tell you a joke about a bed?

It hasn't been made up yet.

Why can't you tell twin witches apart?
Because it's hard to tell which witch is which.

Why didn't the boy want to go to the cemetery?

He didn't want to be caught dead there.

How can you get rich by not saying a word?

Because silence is golden.

Why do moms carry their babies?

Because babies don't carry their moms.

What kind of shower doesn't need water?

A baby shower.

Who are the most patient people?
Doctors.

How do dog catchers get paid?

By the pound.

What do all 18th-century leaders have in common?

They're all dead.

How do you pronounce the capital of Missouri: "Saint Looo-Issss" or "Saint Loueeee"?

"Jefferson City."

What's loud, dangerous, and very boring?

Drilling giant holes.

What kind of baker is best known for making nothing?
A doughnut baker.

What dress cannot be worn?
Address.

Why don't honest people need beds?
They never lie!

When is homework not homework?
When it's turned into the teacher!

I'm round on both sides and high in the middle.
Quite the state!
Ohio.

If April showers bring May flowers,
what do May flowers bring?
Pilgrims.

What kind of school is above college?

High school.

Who always gets the most dates?

A date farmer.

What's as big as Texas but invisible and never moves?

The border around Texas.

If George Washington were alive today,
what would be be most famous for?
For being the oldest man in the world!

Why can't a Canadian woman living in the U.S. be buried in the U.S.?

Because she isn't dead.

In what room would you never find a ghost?

The living room.

Who earns a living by always driving
their customers away?
A taxi driver.

Mr. Green lives in a green house,
Mr. Blue lives in a blue house,
so who lives in a White House?
The president.

What's the most tiring day of the year?
April 1. Everyone just spent
31 days Marching.

Two's company, three's a crowd, so what are
four and five?
Nine.

A surgeon named Hal and a bus driver named Al are both in love with the same woman named Paige. Al needs to go for a long trip of 10 days. Before he left he gave Paige 10 apples. Why? An apple a day keeps the doctor away.

What do you have to do before a friend forgives you for being mean?

Be mean to your friend!

Who makes more money than they get paid?

A money printer.

Who would be most bummed out if they lost 20 pounds?

A British person.

You can crack me, or make me, or tell me, or play me on your friends. What am I?
A joke!

Why are calendars always afraid?

Because their days are numbered.

Why are 1991 pennies worth more than 1990 pennies?

Because 1991 pennies are one more than 1990 pennies.

9
TOUGH ONES

Hard Harbingers of Head-Scratching

If you have it, you want to share it.
If you share it, you no longer have it. What is it?
A secret.

You don't want it, but if you do have it, you don't want to lose it.
What is it?
A lawsuit.

I'm not visible, touchable, or wrong, and it takes three of me to figure out what's left.
What am I?
Right.

You won't soon forget me, no matter how often you question me.
What am I?
The past.

A man has nine children.
Half of them are girls.
How is this possible?
They're all girls.

What do the rich need, the poor have, and if you eat it . . . you'll die?
Nothing.

Those who have it the least don't Know that they have it. And those who have it most wish they had less of it, but not too little or none at all. What is it?
Age.

The more you take, the more you leave behind. What are they?

Footsteps.

Monica's father has three daughters: Maggie, Maddie, and . . . who?

Monica!

What belongs to you, but other people use it more than you do?

Your name.

What can you hold without ever touching?
A conversation.

Mr. and Mrs. Murray have six daughters, and each daughter has one brother.
How many people are in the Murray family?
There are nine Murrays.
The daughters all have the same brother,
so there are six daughters, one son, and Mr. and Mrs. Murray.

What gets broken without being held?
A promise.

A man has married hundreds of women, but he himself has never been married. How's that possible?

He's a priest.

What's always coming but never arrives?

Tomorrow.

What kind of ship has two mates but no captain?
A relationship.

Two boys were born to the same mother,
on the same day,
at the same time, in the same month and year.
But they're not twins.
How's that?
They're two of three triplets.

You can only keep me after you've given me.
What am I?
Your word.

What's hard to find, easy to lose, worth more than
gold,
but doesn't cost anything?
A good friend.

I'm a mother's child but nobody's son.
What am I?
A daughter.

A doctor and a nurse have a baby.
The baby's father is not the doctor, and the mother is
not the nurse.
How is it possible?
The doctor is the mother, and the nurse is
the father.

If your uncle's sister is not your aunt, then who is she?
Your mother.

I'm always in front of you, but you'll never see me.
What am I?
The future.

What has no beginning, middle, or end?
A circle.

What has everyone seen but will never see again?
Yesterday.

A woman sits at home at night with all of the lights off,
and doesn't have any lamps on or candles burning.
But she reads comfortably. How?
She's reading Braille.

Mary gets in the shower, but surprisingly her hair is not wet when she gets out. How is this possible? She didn't turn the water on.

What's always late and is never around right now?

Later.

Why would a hair stylist rather cut the hair of two brunettes than one redhead?

They would get paid more for two haircuts than one.

Paul is 20 years old in 1980, but only 15 years old in 1985. How is this possible?

The dates are 1980 and 1985 B.C.

You're my sister but I am not your sister. Who am I?
Your brother.

How can "L" be greater in size than "XL"?
In Roman numerals.

I happened in the past, remembered now, and headed for the future.
What am I?
History.

Everyone needs it, most will ask for it, some will give it, but almost no one takes it. What is it?
Advice.

The shorter I am, the bigger I am. What am I?
Your temper.

I have a thousand wheels but never move.
It's a lot. What am I?
A parking lot!

Three men rob a store but come out completely
changed.
Yet they continue robbing other stores.
What kind of store did they rob?
A clothing store . . . where they changed clothes.

What is the easiest way to poke a balloon
without popping it?
Poke one that isn't inflated.

Wednesday, Eric and Lindsay went to a restaurant for lunch.
When they were done, they paid for the food and left.
But Eric and Lindsay didn't pay. So who did?
Their friend, Wednesday.

You fill up a bathtub with water, and you have a teaspoon, tablespoon, and a coffee mug.
What is the fastest way to empty the bathtub?
Pull the drain plug.

Megan and Tegan both want to sit behind each other in class, so their teacher arranges them so they're both happy. How did she do it?
They sit back-to-back.

A farmer has three fields.
One of them has 3 bundles of hay, another has 4, and the last has 5.
How many would he have in the first field if he combined all of them in that field?
Just one, he combined them all.

A man and his boss have the same parents, but they aren't siblings.
How is this possible?
He's self-employed.

I make up all books, and yet I'm often sealed.
What am I?
Letters.

What do thieves get for stealing calendars?

12 months.

**What's a question that gets asked often
and has many different answers?**

"What's your name?"

What am I?

A question.